My Name is Chivalry

Ten Principles of Chivalry

authorHOUSE®

AuthorHouse™
1663 Liberty Drive
Bloomington, IN 47403
www.authorhouse.com
Phone: 1 (800) 839-8640

Published by AuthorHouse 06/13/2019

ISBN: 978-1-7283-1093-0 (sc)
ISBN: 978-1-7283-1091-6 (hc)
ISBN: 978-1-7283-1092-3 (e)

Library of Congress Control Number: 2019906090

Contents

About the Author

Donnell Cooper devotes time and resources performing social skill, speaking presentations and etiquette workshops with companies all over the country. He has had the opportunity of speaking to many youth groups and affiliations throughout the country such as the National Basketball Association, Exxon-Mobile, United Way, Young Lawyer's Association, and a vast majority of the grass root community organizations.

While completing his educational studies he found through his thorough research that 80% of most college graduates were not successful with securing jobs due to a lack of social skills. It was at that time when he decided to give back to community and deliver what he calls the necessary Social Skills of Etiquette.

Donnell has motivated and empowered individuals to implement and practice the necessary social skills and graces of etiquette in order to surpass their goals, dreams and aspirations in life. Donnell believes that these necessary social skills and graces of etiquette can cultivate an entire country of people with the capabilities of socializing regardless of their socioeconomic class.

Donnell states, "That etiquette is a chosen Life-Style you choose, not a Life-Style that chooses you".

Donnell has had the opportunity of leading and managing many organizations within his time which have all had a great impact on his life and his future success.

Introduction

When we hear the word chivalry, for many people, the image that instantly forms in our minds is one of an Elizabethan man, a knight in shining amour who is polite, kind and opens doors for people, especially women.

While in some form, this is chivalry, it is not entirely limited to the act of opening doors for people, or helping people out of cars. It is also not limited to a gender or a generation.

Chivalry manifests in different aspects of our lives; in our personal relationship, our work relationship, our table manners, and even what we choose to wear!

Most definitions of chivalry that you will find point out kindness, valor, honor, gallantry, and courtesy, as was the code of the mediaeval knights, especially by men, towards women. Now, times have changed, and people with it. We all have increased social responsibilities towards one another, regardless of gender, culture, or any other factor that could be a divide.

I wrote this book with the purpose of showing just how chivalry can manifest in different situations that we might find ourselves, and how best to navigate such waters to yield the best result; which is one of satisfaction for you, and everyone involved. There is a principle of chivalry for everything that involves another person or more, and this book will show you just how important these principles are.

Chapter One

The Principles of Chivalry When Conducting Business Within the Office Space

When it comes to shared offices spaces, you have to understand that it is not just about you. You have a responsibility to other people who share the space with you, and as such, should be very careful as to what you do, and how it will affect them.

———

Chivalry demands that you put other people into consideration when you talk and act, and in a shared workspace, one thing to be very particular about is not disturbing others with your phone calls. Nobody likes someone who speaks too loudly, especially over the phone. They do not want to be able to hear all the details of your conversation loud and clear while they are trying to get their own work done.

———

If you must make a call in a shared workspace - that is not against any rules, as your job description might demand it of you - be mindful to keep your voice such that the person on the desk next to you can barely make out what you are even talking about. That is the best way to have phone conversations in a shared workspace. Schedule personal conversations that might make you lose your composure, like calls with family and friends for after work hours, and if you must take them during work hours, excuse yourself, step out, and make your call.

———

Your colleagues will find it very distracting if they have to listen to you talk about your last vacation over the phone while they are trying to get work done.

———

Another aspect of workspace chivalry is in your introduction to a colleague, boss or client of your company.

———

In greetings and introduction in a work setting, it is essential that you be as professional as possible, in a way that respects the other person's personal space.

———

For example, if you are to introduce yourself to a client, you do not intrude on their personal space by hugging them when they have extended their hand for a handshake. It is best that you keep all greetings simple, straight to the point and highly professional.

———

Unprofessional is telling them personal facts that you were not asked, and saying things that are generally considered inappropriate in a work setting, or using inappropriate language, like cuss words.

———

While introducing yourself to a client, a new colleague, or anybody in a workplace setting, either the opposite sex (or even the same sex), don't act unprofessionally by sending sexual vibes their way. For example, don't look at them in a lewd, sexual way, or make comments that are laced with sexual innuendos. Some people might even go as far as to touch someone else in sexual way in the work space. A lot of people find this offensive, especially if they have not given their consent- as they should. If you are caught in a position like this, you just might have a sexual assault charge slapped on your face.

———

In a case where the other party is open to such advances, other people in your workspace might find open display of affections distracting, and you have a duty to them as well. So, it will be in the best interest of everybody to have such advances and displays kept for after office hours. In fact, to avoid distractions as such, several companies have laws in place that forbids coworkers from having intimate relationships. If you work in a place as such, you might want to avoid toeing this path, if you don't want to lose your job. If you are not sure what your company says about this, go to your HR department and find out.

———

Another work place etiquette that isn't very discussed is your personal hygiene. It is your duty, to yourself and people you work with, that have to spend a lot of time with you daily that you maintain an impeccable personal hygiene. It is rather difficult to work with, and maintain a decent workplace relationship with someone that has body odor, mouth odor, or worse, both. You will be doing your colleagues, clients and even yourself a great disservice if your hygiene is poor. Nobody will want to work with you, and if they have to, it will certainly not be under the best working conditions, which might even affect their productivity.

———

Take your time to clean up nicely, brush your teeth before work, wear body spray and a cologne that's not too strong. Look nice and clean, and add a great smile to that.

———

Your choice of outfit is also a part of your workspace chivalry. Some companies have a specific way they want their employees to appear. Going against this is not the chivalrous way, and it could even get you a query or two. If the company policy states that their employees should show up at work wearing a suit, don't show up wearing jeans and a tee. It's a direct disregard of the company rule which is generally unacceptable.

———

In keeping with the dressing code of the company, the way you coordinate your outfits also matters. Try to avoid wearing colors that are distracting or just ugly to look at. In everything you do, even down to what colors and prints you decide to wear, you have to consider not just your wants, but how it aligns with the office policies and how it could affect your co-workers. If an outfit choice is too busy, or is possibly distracting, try not to wear it.

———

If your outfit is too tight, or it exposes too much of your body, especially for women (outfits that show the belly, too much cleavage, or too much legs), it might not be proper enough for work. Everyone wants to walk into a room and turn heads, and that's fine. But in a workspace setting, the goal is to maintain your focus and get the job done, and in time. Anything that will deter your co-workers from this, try as much as you can not to do it.

———

Everybody in a workspace has a right to their own personal space, and the chivalrous thing to do is to respect that space. If your coworker has kept a personal item somewhere, for example, if they have kept their lunch in the office kitchen, it is disrespectful to them to take such an item without their knowledge. If you have to touch something in their workspace, let them know before you do so, because you don't know what the implication of your meddling might be. You don't want to mistakenly tamper with a sensitive file on their system while trying to find your way around a system you should not even be using in the first place. Respect them enough to ask for their permission to touch anything of theirs, and if they don't grant it to you, accept their decision with dignity and let it be.

———

Another aspect of workspace chivalry is learning to be a people person. It is understandable that some people might be very introverted, but that doesn't necessarily mean they should have terrible people manners. If you find yourself working with other people, then it is best you learn how to relate well with them. It doesn't necessarily imply that you have to get personal with them and share every detail of your life with them- if you are that comfortable and they are too, that's fine. But on a professional ground, you should have a great relationship with your co-workers. This breeds a healthy work environment where everyone gets along well, helps one another achieve their work goals and generally maintain a good work relationship.

———

If you are generally grumpy and snappy- you're probably wondering why no one wants to work in the same team as you by now, you might want to learn to be patient and more accommodating towards other people, even those that will get on your nerves. Learning how to manage your frustrations correctly is part of work place chivalry. Clients, colleagues, team members, lower staff members, anybody that you come in contact with in your workspace can frustrate you, and it is certainly unprofessional to lash out every time someone frustrates you, or for you to take it out on someone else in your office space. The chivalrous man or woman understands that these things are bound to happen and they equip themselves mentally to handle such when it arises in a polite and professional manner.

———

In all dealings in a workspace, make professionalism your watchword, be courteous to the people you work with and for, and you will see how your work relationship will evolve for the best.

———

Chapter Two

The Principles of Chivalry
When Getting Dressed

The saying that 'you will be addressed as you are dressed' is not a myth at all. In as much as people are advised not to judge a book by its cover, you need to understand that nobody is psychic, so there is a higher probability that you will be judged first by the cover you present, and that is the way you are dressed. If you want to look like a person who knows what they are doing in their field of study, especially at a meeting or a job interview, you have to dress the part.

————

More often than not, people do not have the time to get to know who you are beneath the layering, so if you are looking to impress someone, dress appropriately, and make the job of getting to know you easier and more pleasant, for them.

———

As a rule, one should dress appropriately for whatever occasion they will be attending, or crowd they will be mingling. If for example, one is going for a job interview, it will be inappropriate to dress like the one heading to the club to hang with their friends on a Friday night. The way you are dressed communicates a lot, and in this case, you will be communicating to your interviewers that you do not respect them enough to dress appropriately for the occasion, and that is not going to work well in your favor.

———

If you are going out on a date with someone, and they take the pain of making a reservation, and all the other things that go with asking someone out on a date, the least you can do, if you accept to go with them, is to dress well for the occasion.

———

Your outfit choice is an expression of your true self, and you have the power to express your sense of style as you chose. It is also important that you hold yourself accountable when making your outfit choices, and consider the people around you. In as much as you want to express your right to be expressive with your style, be sure that your outfit choice is not obscene such that it offends the people around you, or that it deliberately flouts a rule, or two.

———

If you live in an area that frowns upon sagging of pants for men, and showing excessive cleavage for women, for as long as you live there, it is chivalrous that you adhere to those rules.

———

Something that always pays off is to always dress respectably and in a decent manner. Not only do you look better, people will feel better in your company. Really, something as simple as how you are dressed can decide if people will like you or stay away from you.

―――――

How many people do you admire that do not dress well? Think about it.

―――――

Some people are of the opinion that looking good is vanity, and maybe they are right, but who said vanity is a terrible thing? Looking good is very important, especially if you don't stay locked up in your house all day. What is being implied is that if you go out, if you have dealings with people, then it is in fact important that you look good. Looking good is not something that only a few people can achieve, or something that only a few people are entitled to. Neither is looking good something that has to be an expensive venture. As a social experiment, you can try something. On days you are feeling a little bit down, go to your wardrobe, select an outfit that looks great on you, get dressed and go out. The experiment is to determine whether or not you'll feel a little better. In most cases, you will find that you will feel better, even if it's just a bit. Chivalry is not something you express to people alone; it is also service done to the self.

———

You deserve good things- tell yourself that, and one of those things is to adorn with yourself with the best of what you can afford. A lot of emphasis is placed on the word 'afford'. Dress within your budget, in as much as you want to look good, don't break the bank, or run into a debt.

———

Ever heard the saying that one should dress like the person they want to meet? This is the less popular way of the saying, "dress like you want to be addressed". If you are gunning for success, you must understand that opportunities can come anytime. You never can tell who you'll meet on your way out. It could very well be your next big client or your first major investor. So, ask yourself, "who do I want to meet while I'm in town today?" If you aspire to meet one of your mentors, then wear something you want to be seen in by your mentor. If you want to meet an investor, dress up in such a way that if you do meet one, your appearance will not put them off. The energy you send forth is what comes back to you, remember that. This is part of chivalry that you do for yourself, in terms of how the way you are dressed could impact your life.

———

Do you know that caring about your appearance teaches responsibility? Well, it does. A lot of details goes into dressing sharply, and if you are able to pay attention to them, observe and maintain them, there is a higher chance that you will be responsible. Having to keep track of which shirt requires ironing, which shoes require to be polished, and planning your outfit ahead of time reinforces a mental habit of coordination, planning, attention to details and organization that can translate to great skills to possess in a work environment. If you are bringing great skills as such to any team, you will be a valuable member of such a team.

————

Another aspect of chivalry while dressing is to dress appropriately for the job. For example, if you are going to the gym, the right thing to do will be to wear gym outfits. Wearing a dress, for example could cause possible harm to not just you but the other gym users. If you are going to a place that will require that you do some measure of physical labor, ensure that you are properly outfitted for such. It is not right that your outfit be the reason why you can't get the job done. If anything, your choice of clothing should be empowering, and not serve as a hindrance. If it is, then you are clearly doing something wrong.

————

Do you know what looks good on you? Do you know what colors work best with your skin tone? Do stripes or patterns suit you? These are things you should know, because to a large extent, they help dictate what you should wear, and what is advisable that you don't wear. Again, knowing details like this is not being vain, rather, you can think of it as information gathering. Information that you will then make use of to select an outfit when you're out on your next date, or when you're going for your next job interview.

———

There is such a thing as indecent exposure, and if you are not in the right scene for such, you could get into some amount of trouble for exposing so much of your body. In most cases, keeping it classy and decent does the job.

———

Dressing well does not have to be extravagant, or expensive. You do not have to break the bank to look good. Just combine your colors right, and keep the clothes clean.

———

Clean clothes are another important factor. Stepping out in dirty clothes is a burden on everyone that encounters it, because they have to deal with the bad odor that the dirty clothes have. It will not matter how expensive your outfit is, if your clothing is dirty, or if a nasty smell permeates from you, no one will notice that you are well dressed. It will not take a lot to make sure that your clothes are properly dry cleaned and well ironed. Not only your clothes need to be cleaned up, your body has to be clean as well. Maintain proper personal hygiene- take a bath, brush your teeth and wear body spray, you will be doing yourself, and everyone you meet a world of good. No matter how simple you choose to dress, keep it clean!

———

Well presented men and woman complement each other when dressed appropriately. If a lady were to be approached by two men in one single night, one well dressed, and the other shabbily dressed, she is most likely going to pay more attention to the well-dressed man at first. Generally, people prefer to be seen with other people that are well dressed, not that anyone can blame them. So, if you want the people you associate with to actually want to be seen with you, dress like someone that people want to be seen with.

———

Chivalry in dressing somehow translates to chivalry in several areas of one's life, from professional, to personal life. This just goes to show that how we are dressed influences several things in our lives, and as such, a lot of attention should be paid to it.

———

Chapter Three

The Principles of Chivalry When Making Life Decisions

In relationships, there are certain decisions that are not entirely up to you alone to make, as your significant other will also be affected one way or another. It is only polite that in making such decisions, you inform them, listen to their opinions and then find a way to strike a balance between what both parties want in case there is a difference in opinion.

———

Being selfish in a relationship is not chivalrous in any way or form, neither is it healthy to the progress of the relationship. Being courteous is one of the codes of the medieval knighthood system that birthed chivalry in the first place, and an outright disregard to the opinion and feelings of your significant other is not courteous.

———

If you have to make any major life changing decisions that will affect not just you, but your partner as well, then courtesy demands that you inform them about it. And by inform, I don't mean call them over the phone after you have acted upon the decision, or tell them in passing that you have done something as big as, say, sold the house, for example.

———

The best way, the 'knightly' way to go about such things is to sit down with them, discuss your plans, ask for their opinions, and together, come up with a decision as a single unit. Working together as a single unit in a relationship is the height of chivalry in the relationship. Knowing that the opinion of the other person counts, and respecting them as well, is indeed a mark of chivalry.

———

A true gentleman not only opens his partner's doors, but also informs them before he makes any major decisions, and a true lady does the same.

———

As much as possible, it is better not to put your significant other in a tight spot. Of course, it is inevitable sometimes, but do not make a habit out of it. One of the marks of chivalry in a relationship is reducing your partner's burden, easing their tasks and generally making life as easy and smooth sailing for them as possible.

———

One of the best ways to do this is to always make adequate plans for whatever you intend to do that might affect them in one way or another. For example, if you are going on a trip, before you make final travel arrangements (of course, you should have informed your partner already you will be making a trip), put the right plans in place before you finalize your travel plans.

———

For example, if it is your responsibility to have the cleaners come clean your shared apartment and you pay them, then before you finalize plans to travel, set things in motion such that they can still come clean while you are away, and get their payment. Do not just pack up, leave, and assume that your partner will handle everything you leave behind.

———

They might be able to handle it, but you have to inform them first. You do not know if they have plans of theirs that your inconsiderate behavior might disrupt.

———

In all choices you make while in a relationship, bear in mind that you are not thinking for only yourself, and the outcome of your choices will affect not just you.

————

Asides from the relationship you have with your significant other, there is the relationship with your family and friends. Whatever decision you make reflects on them as well, if you have a great relationship with them, that is. These people have a reputation of theirs, and if you do something that's very bad, your actions might dent that reputation terribly. In as much as your life is yours to live, and yours alone, you cannot in the real sense of things make decisions completely independent of anyone in your life. Your choices, actions and even inactions reflects on the people in your life. Therefore, put them into consideration when you make decisions and choices. This is not saying that you should put yourself in a box and then live your life completely dependent on what people will say, and what they will think about the things you do. Not everybody's opinion about your life matters, and even the ones that matter, you still have to weigh the odds. You might not always do what pleases your friends and family, but you owe it to them that you weigh the odds of your actions and the impact it might have on them before you make some moves. So, even if there is a possibility that they would get hurt, you could find a way to mitigate them from it and protect them as much as you can.

———

The world is crawling with selfish people that pay no mind to how their choices affect other people, and a chivalrous person isn't one of them and more of such people are needed.

———

What a lot of people have failed to realize is that every choice they make, every decision they make has a ripple effect that affects not just the people they know, but the ones they don't know as well.

———

For example, if you chose to drink and drive, you could end up hitting an unsuspecting stranger that's trying to cross the road. If that person gets hurt, or worse, dies, the person's life and their family's life will be seriously affected, and not in a good way. This is not exactly a major life decision, but even the little things count. A single thoughtless action as such as the possibility of reshaping another person's life, which is why one has to be extra careful when they make decisions. Consider the different possible outcomes and if at the end of the day you still decide to do it, then it means you are ready to deal with whatever consequences your actions bring.

———

When you make life decisions, add a dash of chivalry by considering not just how it affects your present state but also your future and the people in it. Instant gratification is enjoyable, but it is momentary and eventually the buzz fades away. When that buzz fades away, and you are back to the reality of things, it is important that whatever decision you made reflects who you are and what your values are. They should be choices that glorify you, honor you and ultimately makes you happy. If you make a choice that makes you think, 'if I had known, I'd have been more careful', and it puts you in some measure of trouble, then you have not been chivalrous in your decision making. Recklessness is not one of the traits of a chivalrous person. But, bear in mind that a person can make mistakes. It's a part of life, and nobody is immune to them. So you are bound to make various levels of mistakes while making life decisions. You will make mistakes that delay you, maybe even hurt your significant other, or your family and friends, that's fine. But, mistakes are only a good thing when you learn from them and you make sure that it never happens again. If you keep making the same mistake in your decision making, over and over again and you never learn, then you have to check yourself.

———

A chivalrous man or woman knows to own their mistakes in life decisions, and embrace it, for only then will there be any form of progress, and that's the ultimate goal- Progress. Choices that one makes should generally bring some measure of progress to their lives, and push them towards something in particular. So whatever decisions you make that will not positively affect pushing you in said direction, you might want to reconsider it.

———

In making life decisions and life plans, a chivalrous person is not afraid of being told 'no'. They understand that not all doors will open to them, whether they chose to knock on that door doesn't matter- Some doors will just not open for them. It is a virtue of the chivalrous person to know when to cut his losses and move on to another door.

———

In making life decisions, the little details count. Attention to the barest amount of details is one of the attributes of a chivalrous person, and it is usually reflected when they make life choices. A big plan, an intelligent plan could still become a terrible disaster if proper attention is not paid to the little details that surrounds it. So, when thinking about the major things to put in place, the options you want to pick from and things as such, consider the little pieces of information that surrounds a thing before you finally decide on what to do.

——————

Finally, as with a lot of aspects of chivalry, patience finds its way to this area as well. Rushed decisions are not advisable, especially when they are life changing ones. Relax, take a few steps back, be patient and then think things through very well. The quality of your life will definitely be better when you don't just rush into everything head on.

——————

Chapter Four

The Principles of Chivalry
When Going to Dinner

If you get an invite to have dinner at the house of a family member, friend, a boss, or anyone that invites you to dinner, really, the first thing to do is accept the invite. RSVPing is very important, especially if it is a formal invite. Your host expects that you RSVP, and if you don't, they assume that you will not show up so they might not make adequate preparations for you. If you end up showing up without RSVPing, it might be inconvenient for them. Of course they can't turn you back, but they will also not be able to say, 'hey, sorry, but we don't have enough food to give you.'

———

If you cannot make it, tell them in time that you will not be able to make it, and apologize for it. When giving a reason for not attending, don't just say, 'Sorry, I can't make it.', that sounds as if you just don't want to attend their dinner- even if you don't, it doesn't have to be so apparent. Give a reason for not attending, such as, "I'm sorry, but I'll not be able to attend your dinner, I have to make a work trip that day."

———

In giving your excuse, keep it short and simple. A succinct explanation does the job better than a long convoluted tale. If you delve into the former, at some point it might begin to look like you are simply making silly excuses for not actually wanting to attend. Keep it simple and straight forward. At the end of it, apologize profusely, and if you can, have a gift sent over to the host on the day of the dinner, like a bottle of wine or some flowers.

———

If you do accept the invite, endeavor not to show up late, and if you find yourself running late because of some unexpected circumstances - those happen - call to let them know.

———

It really is just about respecting your hosts enough to stick to their plans, and letting them know if things do not work out as planned for you.

———

The gentlemanly/lady thing to do when you do show up is to bring something along with you. They might not demand it of you, neither might they expect it from you, but they will be happy if you show up with a bottle of wine or a bowl of chicken salad, for example.

———

Again, dress well for the occasion. If your host has selected a dress code, abide by it, and if not, keep it neat and presentable.

———

Another thing to be mindful of are your table manners. Nobody likes to eat around a person who shoves too much food in his or her mouth, or a person who talks with food in the mouth. Eat with your mouth closed, eat slowly and do not talk while there is food in your mouth.

———

If your table manners are lacking, you just might not get another invite, and you might even lose a bit of your host's respect. Other table manners include stretching your hands over another person's food, using your hands to eat when you are supposed to eat with your cutlery, eating noisily and spilling food everywhere. You might enjoy eating this way, but other people find it bothersome, and borderline disgusting. In fact, everyone should have proper table manners, as they do not know what kind of company they will find themselves, and proper manners will take you places.

———

There is a system to the way food is served around a dinner table, depending on whether or not it is a formal setting. Either ways, wait your turn and don't create a nuisance around the table because you want to quickly be served. If the food is being passed around and you are serving yourself, be considerate of other people on the table. Serve a reasonable portion of food on your plate and then pass the platter. If at the end of the day there is some leftover and you still want another helping, you can ask the host for it. Don't just assume that you can eat it just because there is more left. Ask first.

————

As much as you can, engage in conversations that are going on around the table - without food in your mouth, of course - and try not to act as if attending was not your choice. Be nice, friendly and kind to the people that have so graciously opened their home to you, and their other guests.

————

At the end of the meal, if you can, offer to help clear the table and clean the dishes. Being kind and helpful has a way of endearing people to you, and it will be better if you are remembered as the nice guy or lady who brought wine and helped with the dishes, than the loud eater who didn't know food should stay on the plate, and not on the floor.

———

If alcohol is served at the table, you might want to go light on the drinking, especially if you cannot hold your liquor. It is of poor taste, and down right unchivalrous to get drunk at dinner, especially when it is not over. Even if it is over, it is best to stay safe and not get drunk. Alcohol being served is not the problem. The problem is that drunk people are not exactly pleasant to be around. If you get drunk, there is the possibility that you say nasty things, a lot of things you should not say, or that you embarrass yourself and the host in one form or another.

———

In fact, if you will be driving, stay completely away from the wine. One glass could easily turn into two, and before you know it, you are swaying slightly on your feet.

———

If you are in a terrible mood on the day of the dinner and you know that there is a high probability that you will take it out on someone at the dinner table, then send a message to your host or call them to apologize and let them know that you will not be attending the dinner. It is not fair to your host and every other person in attendance for you to go over there and start taking out your frustration, or acting out your mood on them. The best thing is to excuse yourself politely, and if you are sure that you can handle it, then get dressed and have fun.

Treat the other guests of your host with utmost respect, even if they are not your friends and you have never met them before. Be kind and attentive to them and you never can tell, you just might make a new friend or two.

If you have a plus one that you want to bring to dinner, and your invite is for one person, it is best that you tell your host before you just show up with someone else. This mostly applies to formal settings, but in cases of family and friends as host, if you are sure that they'll not mind you showing up with someone else unannounced, then it's fine.

———

Usually, when someone invites other people to their home for dinner, it is usually for a reason- to celebrate a success, to discuss important matters, or to just catch up with an old friend. Usually, the reason is apparent in the manner and circumstances of the invite. Help your host to attain this goal by contributing to conversations around the table. Don't just nod and smile, or answer questions in a curt manner as if you were forced to attend. If you are going to be that way, then it is best that you don't accept the invite to attend.

———

This chapter says, 'Principle of Chivalry when going to dinner', but we will also hint on some of the principles of chivalry when you have guests over for dinner.

—————

As a host, you have a duty to your guests to feed them and cater to their needs while they are in your house. If you are not certain what your guests like, or whether they have allergies or not, ask them, and tell them to give their response along with their RSVP. You might put them in an awkward position when you place a bowl of salad they can't eat in front of them. Most people are too polite to refuse it, so they'll most likely have to shove down food in an unpleasant manner all through the dinner- not fun at all.

—————

You also have a responsibility to your guests. If you are serving alcohol, assign designated drivers and make sure that they don't drink. This way, you can be sure that when your guests leave your house they will not be driving head on into a tree.

———

Remember to smile at your guests, show them where to hang their coats and generally make them feel comfortable and welcomed in your home, after all, you did invite them into your home, it is the least you can do.

———

Chapter Five

The Principles of Chivalry When Making The Right Choices

Choices are a very personal thing, and although they are influenced by several things, it is important that you do not allow the power of your choice be taken away from you.

———

While you are exercising the power of your choice, be aware of your responsibility towards other people, especially those your choices may affect. There is such a thing as recklessness and insubordination even in the making of choices, and one of the ways it presents is in truth telling during communication.

———

Honesty is a code of the knight, and so nothing that disregards this is an act of chivalry. In your communication with others, be as truthful as you can. When you tell lies to someone, what you are essentially saying is that they are not worthy of knowing the truth, that it is fine for you to toy with their emotions with a lie because they do not matter that much anyway. People do not like to feel this way, and they should not have to feel this way.

———

In all your dealings with people, tell the truth. It is best not to put yourself in a situation where you will need to lie to another person to get out of it. If your ways are proper, and you do things the right way, you will not need to tell lies to cover up for anything. The right choices will not require that you lie about them.

———

Still on the matter of making right choices, do not let the choices you make put you in such a position that you will embarrass yourself. Choices are such powerful things, and it is no wonder that many people try to suppress other people and take away that power from them. When you exercise your power to make a choice, be careful with it. Treat it like a loaded gun that you do not want to fire randomly in a crowded room, least you hurt someone.

———

While you are mindful not to hurt others, leave some space for self-preservation. You have a duty to yourself first, before anything else. So, make sure that your choices do not embarrass you, get you into an unwholesome situation or soil your reputation.

———

Your power to choose should give you freedom, it should give you wings to fly and be the best version of yourself. But if it only gets you in messy situations, and makes life complicated and awkward for you, then you are doing something terribly wrong, and it is time to reconsider those choices.

———

There is such a thing as responsibility in choice making. We have discussed how your choices should affect you; there is also the part of how it affects others. Reckless choice making can endanger the people around you. While you are thinking about the effect of your choices on yourself, you should also put into consideration the effect it will have on other people.

———

In making choices, you should learn to train and tame your emotions. Deep down, what we all just want to do is to sleep, eat, watch TV all day, or play video games all day, and do those other things that are our basic human instincts. Nobody really wants to make the hard decisions, or the hard choices. Emotions are basic things that are not as intelligent as we have lead ourselves to believe. If we let emotions alone rule our lives, they will drive us straight into a tree and leave us to crash and burn. They don't exactly consider the consequences of their actions, they just act. Oh, they are also chronic over reactors. You know how you feel when you are mad at someone and you just want to rip their head off, or when something bad happens to you, you just want to run away and hide from everyone? That is your emotions acting out what it does best.

———

Gratefully, our brain has developed logic and the ability to weigh the odds and consequences of every action and choices. But, your emotions and logic are constantly waging wars against each other, and for your own good, logic should win more often than emotions.

———

This is the part where emotional intelligence is introduced. Emotional intelligence is not only applicable when dealing with other people and how we react to things that happen around us. In the choices we make and how we make them, our emotional intelligence is reflected. For example, if you have a test coming up in school for a course you absolutely dislike, your natural instinct will be not to study for the test at all. You will rather sleep than stay up all night studying a course you hate. But an emotionally intelligent person knows that if they don't study for a test, they will fail, and of they fail, it could greatly impact their result and maybe even their future. So, despite the fact that they don't enjoy it, they still do it because they have weighed the odds and have decided that it will be better for them to study. So, they do it. In essence, chivalry is not complete without emotional intelligence.

———

When making choices, you have to understand the concept of weighing values. There are numerous types of values- emotional value, financial value, physical value, social value, etc. in making choices, weigh your values appropriately, and not just how it matters now, in the short term, but in the long term as well. To be able to do this, you have to first of all be able to define what your values are, in all aspects of your life. Know what matters to you and what is just white noise and be able to make a clear distinction between them. Now this part is rather difficult because for the most part, people are not able to make such clear distinctions, or see things clearly enough to know what matters most and what is in fact white noise.

———

Consider it a code of chivalry to know how to filter through everything around you and be able to separate the ones that matter from the ones that don't. It takes a lot of practice, patience and introspection to get to a stage where you have defined yourself enough to figure out the most important things to you and the things that add more value to you. Nobody was born with this ability; neither can you develop it overnight. It is something that has to be learned, practiced and then relearned again over and over until it becomes instinctual.

———

You have to master the art of discipline in your life if you want to be truly chivalrous in making important life choices. Discipline comes in all forms- from not indulging yourself on all wimps to ensuring that you strike off everything on your to-do list in good time. If you can successfully master discipline, you will be able to apply it in making the right choices, from what you should eat, what you should wear to what career path is best for you.

––––––

Ask yourself when you make a choice. "Am I choosing this because it makes for a better story and it will look better on paper, or because it is what I really want?" How you answer that question says a lot about you and how you observe the codes of chivalry.

––––––

A truly chivalrous person does not make choices because it makes for a better story, or because people will like them more if they do that thing while it puts them in a state of inner turmoil. Remember that in as much as you should strive not to hurt people with your choices, you should not live your life solely based on their approval and on what they will find more enjoyable. If you do this, you will have effectively placed yourself in a cage of your own making and then proceed to live the rest of your life based on what they want. This is no way to live! The old medieval knights lived a life of service, truly, but they were happy with what they were doing. They were happy with their choices, and for every sacrifice they made, they did it with joy in their heart. Can you say the same about the choices you are making? If it doesn't make you happy, don't do it. It really is just as simple as that. Be considerate, think about other people, yes. All these things are important and truly honorable. But don't forsake your inner peace for honor. There is no honor in that at all.

———

To make choice making easier for you, surround yourself with people that you have meaningful relationships with. The people you relate with greatly affect the quality of your life. If you surround yourself with people that edify and motivate you, you will find that certain things will fall in place better for you, and when you find yourself in a fix and some choices are seeming hard to make, you can trust that you'll get help from the people in your circle, and that's the best kind of circle to have.

———

True chivalry knows to be considerate and kind, both to self and to others, even in your decision-making.

———

Chapter Six

The Principles of Chivalry
When Attending a Party

A general rule of thumb when attending a party is to know that if the party is not for you, then it is not about you. Many people forget this, and make the whole thing about them. Do not be one of those people.

———

If you get an invite to a party and you are required to RSVP, ensure that you do that in time. The whole point of RSVP's is to help the party organizers know the number of guests to expect and how to prepare for them. Not RSVP'ing at all or not doing it in time is a little impolite to your hosts. The moment you get an invite to a party, RSVP to confirm your attendance, and if you will not be able to make it, let them know not to expect you at all. If you will be going along with a date, and your invite does not include a plus one, confirm with your host if it's fine for you to bring someone with you so that they can cater for an extra guest. Imagine if everyone that was invited to a party of 15 brings an extra along without informing the host. Surely, it will be weird if you are asked to split a can of beer.

———

Now, if you do decide to attend and you RSVP, do not show up at the party empty handed. Bring a gift along with you, even if that is just a bottle of wine. Showing up at a party without a gift might not have you sent out of the party or anything like that, but it certainly makes you look better when you show up with a gift, no matter how small.

———

A bottle of wine and a bouquet of flowers are the usual gifts, and those are fine, but you can get more creative with your gifts. If you know that your host has a sweet tooth, gift them a box of chocolate, or their favorite type of candy. Scented candles and center pieces for the home are also great gifts. There is no rule against giving homemade gifts, so if that's what you can afford, then don't be ashamed to present it. In fact, a well baked apple pie is just as great a gift.

————

Another act of chivalry to practice when going to a party is adhering to the dress code of the party, or wearing something that goes in line with the selected theme of the party. If you are not sure if there is a dress code, ask your host ahead of time to save you any form of embarrassment. Imagine showing up for a white and black formal themed event wearing jeans and t-shirt. You might feel out of place in such a setting, and you will definitely look weird in the pictures! If the invite you got does not mention a dress code, ask the host. It will save you from a lot of future embarrassment.

————

If your host then tells you the dress code, as much as you can, try to adhere to it. Some people think abiding by a dress code is lame, and lets you blend in with the crowd when they will rather stand out. What they fail to remember is that the party is not about them, as I have mentioned earlier. If the host is throwing an all-white party and you are clearly aware of this but you choose to wear all black instead, you have crossed a line of simple party etiquettes. In selecting a theme or dress code for their party, your host clearly had a vision in mind, and they are relying on their guests to help them bring their vision to life.

It is unfair to them if you sabotage their vision, either intentionally or unintentionally by your choice of outfit. So, try to be a good person, respect the desires of your host and be a model guest. If you find it uncomfortable, you either excuse yourself from the party, or stick with it for the few hours you will be there after which you can go home and do what you like.

The best guests to any party are those that are punctual, you just ask anybody that has ever thrown a party. Try as much as possible not to be more than 15 minutes late, at the most. Don't arrive too early either as they host might be getting ready and doing general preps. The only reason you have to arrive early is if you are helping out with the preparations, and in that case, you absolutely have to arrive early- especially if you have promised to help. It can be quite annoying and awkward when a guest arrives way before the party is scheduled to start. Like, what do they do while the host is getting dressed? Awkward!

———

During the party, there is usually something the host has to do to endure that everything goes smoothly. Offer to help out- they are mostly likely going to say no, but offer nonetheless. If the host looks stressed, insist on helping them pass around drinks, finger foods, directing guests to the main party area, or any other thing that can ease their task and help them enjoy their party as well.

———

One of the points of attending a party is to meet new people and possibly make new, meaningful connections. Move around, talk to other people, or at least make an effort to, and try to have fun. You will make everything awkward if you are being rude to people that try to strike up a conversation with you, or you are giving off a certain vibe that screams 'please stay away from me'. Don't be a party pooper for your host and other people in attendance, be a good sport as much as you can.

———

If you are going to be at a party, then really be there. Don't be at a party, especially those small intimate ones where people can feel your 'absence'. A lot of us are used to checking our phones every few seconds, refreshing our social media pages and replying to IM's. If you decide to attend a party, then be there in every way that counts- physically, mentally, psychologically and every way that counts. It is not enough that your physical body is there, when you really are having an online discussion on Twitter or Facebook.

Have fun. Yes, it is a requirement. Your host wants to know that their guests are having fun and enjoying themselves. Help your host by actually having fun, or at least, putting genuine efforts into it. Again, don't be a party pooper. Participate in whatever games and activities your host has put in place. Be a good sport and have fun. You don't want your host thinking they have not done enough, or that their party is terrible.

Compliment your host on their party. Let them know that their food is great, or that their dress is lovely. If they have invited you into their home, compliment their home. It is not being a kiss ass; it is just the polite thing to do.

––––––

No matter how plentiful the food and drinks are, don't overindulge such that you start throwing up around the house, or you have to be helped home. Enjoy yourself, but in moderation. Don't eat so much that other guests start to give you a bad look. Your host wants you to feel welcome in the space they have created, but you should not take advantage of it. Remember that no matter how comfortable they try to make you feel, it is still not your house and you should comport yourself with some modicum of respect.

––––––

At the end of the party, refrain from asking for left overs. If it is offered to you, then you can accept it, but otherwise, it just comes off strange to ask for leftovers from the party. If you really like a meal that was served, just ask for the recipe instead. That is classier and socially appropriate than straight up asking for leftovers.

———

If you use your host's toilet and or bathroom, be sure to leave it as you met it- hopefully, clean and well organized. There is nothing as annoying as having to deal with a dirty toilet that your guests could not be bothered to keep clean after throwing a party. It is not only rude, it is also disgusting, so don't be one of those guests that mess up the toilets for their hosts. Clean up after yourself- flush the toilet, drop the toilet seat, put the tissue paper back where you took it from, dispose of any used tissue properly, close any tap you open and don't forget to close the door when you step out.

———

Before you leave a party, be sure to tell your host that you're leaving and thank them for the great time. Whether you leave earlier, or when the party ends, still talk to the host and thank them for the great time. Try to exit gracefully by walking out as you came in- sober and alert. Simply means that you should not get drunk, and you should certainly not over eat.

———

Chapter Seven

The Principles of Chivalry While Dating

If you are taking a person out on a date, there are etiquettes that apply. Dates can take several forms, but we will focus on a restaurant date. If you ask someone out on a dinner date, there are things expected of you.

―――――

First thing you have to do of course is to pick a place, and in doing so, you have to make some research. This research includes finding out the standard of the restaurant. Do they serve great food there? Do they have excellent customer service? Are their surroundings neat? Is it somewhere your date would like to encounter people? The answers to these questions will help you determine where to take your date. It is completely unbecoming for your date to dress very regally, expecting to dine in a place with fine surroundings, only for them to find themselves in a shack in some unwholesome place.

———

Another thing to add to your research list is the menu list of whatever restaurant you are considering. Imagine finding out they do not have a vegetarian menu when you are already there, and your date adheres to a strict vegetarian diet. One word, awkward!

———

To avoid such awkward situations, do an extensive research on the restaurant if you have not been there before. Even if you have been there, be certain that it suits not only your needs, but that of your date as well.

———

Another important thing to remember is reservations making. Always, always call ahead to make sure there will be a table waiting for you. It is rather embarrassing to both you and your date to get to a restaurant and have them tell you that you cannot eat there because you did not have the foresight to make a reservation ahead of time. You might not be so fortunate as to find another decent restaurant to dine around, so make the right moves.

———

If you ask someone out on a date and you find yourself running late, call to inform them, give them a reason and let them know when you'll likely be there. Also, if you will not be showing up at all, do tell them, preferably before the day of the date. In some parts of the world, leaving people stood up is a crime - well, it should be. It is rude and inconsiderate, and those two are not in the code of chivalry.

———

In fact, both the person asked out on the date and the asker should not show up late, and if they find themselves running late, the right thing to do is to call the other party, and when you show up eventually, be sure to apologize. People do not like to have their time wasted.

————

A gentleman should open the door for his date, hold out seats for her, and ask her what she wants to eat, instead of taking the choice from her hands. These things might seem old school and out of style, but good manners never ever grow old, as they are in fact timeless.

————

Whichever side of a date you find yourself, ensure you are companionable, friendly, and just try to have fun, so long as you have agreed to be there.

————

While you are out on a date, keep your phone on silent and keep it out of reach from you. It is rude to your date if you are on the phone half the time you are on the date. If you absolutely have to take a phone call, ask for your date's permission to do so, and then keep it very short. But, try as much as possible not to use your phone when you are out on a date.

————

Don't show up to your date drunk, or even slightly drunk. It is never a good idea to show up to your date after 'a few glasses of wine'. Wait till your date progresses before you start drinking at all, and if you must drink hard, it should be a unanimous decision between you and your date. For example, you could both decide to do shots together as a part of your date, but don't do shots before your date and then show up swaying on your feet and reeking of alcohol. It is unattractive and impolite.

————

There is this thing going on now where there is a disagreement as to who should get the bills after a date. If the date was your idea, then you should offer to pay the bills before your date can even say anything. This doesn't mean you will be responsible for every tab if you both decide to see each other again. It's just good manners to pick the tab if you did the asking. It also shows that you are generous and the person you are out on a date with might appreciate that more. If they insist that you split the bill though, then that's something else. But, don't ask that they split the bill upfront if you asked them. This is why you should pick a location that is friendly to your pocket but that is still very elegant and of good taste.

———

The whole point of going out on a date with someone is to get to know them more and have fun with them. If it is a first date, you want to show them that you actually care about them and you will like to know them. You can do this by asking the right questions. To make things less awkward, you can prepare these questions before the date, and then ask them. Make conversation a two-way street. If they ask you something about yourself and you answer, don't just end it at that- ask them something about themselves as well. Conversations generally flow better when at least one of you is a great listener. If you have done the asking, then it falls on you to be very attentive. Pay attention to them, to the things they say, even the smallest expressions they make. If you really like the person and you are looking to making them like you, you might want to practice this. People like to be made to feel like they are seen, respected and valued. Really paying attention to them is one of the ways of showing this, and if you're doing it correctly, your efforts will not go unnoticed.

———

Honesty will earn you a lot of points- at the end of the day, your date might not like those things you were honest about, but you will be saving yourself from a future disaster by telling the truth at the moment anyway. Don't lie about things you are asked, even the littlest things. You might really get to like one another and decide to take things to the next level. Imagine finding out down the line that you have built everything based on a lie!

———

Dates, sometimes usually come with some form of pressure, usually as to what the other person wants in relation to what you want. Spare both of you that trouble by talking about what expectations the both of you have about that date. If you are just looking for a fun way to spend the evening, that may or may not lead anywhere, tell them this so that the both of you don't feel pressured all night into being who you are not.

———

Keeping an open mind is a part of chivalry. In a world that is too judgmental about everyone and everything in it, the chivalrous man or woman learns to keep an open mind. Of course, it is important that you have a standard and you stick to it, but it is also important that you learn to keep an open mind. Your date could be totally different from you in certain areas, that doesn't make them terrible people, or someone you can't have close relations with. If your date appears to have some qualities that you don't admire, before you completely write them off, find out if there is something about them that you actually like. You never can tell, you just might find them very admirable in other areas of their life, so much so that your initial reservation does not even matter.

————

After the date, quite a number of things could happen, and you can control what happens. If you and your date hit it off and you decide to take it back to either one of your apartments, be sure that there are no mixed signals involved and that you are reading whatever signals they are throwing your way correctly. A lot of men have been charged with sexual harassment allegations because they read the signal their date was sending them wrongly. Better still, to avoid sad stories, be clear about your wants and expectations, and ask them about theirs as well. If they want the same thing as you do, then all is well. If they don't, don't force anything on them as you could get into trouble with the law for it.

————

You are both adults, so if you both decide to take the date back to your house, be very clear about your expectations. Never assume anything- that is a rule of thumbs, and it has literally saved lives.

———

After a date, if you have not enjoyed yourself as much as you expected and you will not like to go on a date with that person again, you don't have to be rude about it. A gentleman/ gentlelady knows not to make people feel like 'a piece of shit', they usually know how to let people down easily. And if you do want to hang out with the person again, be sure to tell just how much you enjoyed their company and how much you'll want to go out them again.

———

Chapter Eight

The Principles of Chivalry When Attending a Job Interview

Remember that thing I said about dressing how you want to be addressed? Well, it applies here too. One of the things that interviewers look out for in a job interview is the way the interviewees are dressed.

––––––

It will not matter how perfect a match you are for the position, if you do not look the part. Nobody is going to give you the job. You actually have to convince them you are what they are looking for, and the first way to do that is to dress for success. When you walk into the interviewing room, you want to capture their attention and make them want to listen to what you have to say. That is what dressing for success helps you do.

––––––

So, how do you dress for success? The secret is in picking the right colors and the right fit. There are about four colors advisable for you to stick with in selecting an outfit when you are going for a job interview - black, brown, grey, navy blue. These colors are solid, they are not so loud that they distract the eyes and they do a better job at making you look professional.

———

Wearing yellow to an interview for example not only distracts people, it will also make you look like a clown. An incompetent clown. Now, if you show up in a black suit looking dapper and clean, it is very likely people will want to listen to what you have to say.

———

Ill-fitting clothes are not attractive, and they sure will not score you points with your interviewers, as they will make you look scruffy.

———

Shine your shoes, iron your clothes and look neat and well put together. Not even the right colors can help you if you are dirty and scruffy.

———

Make sure your personal hygiene is not non-existent. No company will employ a person that shows up without taking a shower, or shaving their beards, if they appear clean shaven. Neither will they employ someone that has a terrible mouth odor. It cannot be over emphasized that personal hygiene is important in every area of one's life and it is not one of those things that is overrated. If you smell terribly, no one will want to work with you, or hire you. It is that simple. If you have been out of a job for a while, and as such you have been mostly indoors, wasting away, when you have a job interview, clean up nicely and show up with your best side on full display. Truly, it is what is in your head that truly matters, but no one will come close enough to find out when you reek terribly.

———

Another thing to be mindful of is your cologne use. Do not say, 'I sweat when I get nervous, I don't want to put people off with the smell of sweat', and then for this reason, you slap on enough cologne for three people. That overwhelming assault on their nasal senses can and will most likely put people off just as much as body odor would. Use colognes that have good fragrances, don't just opt for any kind of cologne- just any cologne will not do. Something with a sweet and mild fragrance. If it has a strong fragrance, try not to spray it all over your body. The aim is not to enter a room and choke the people in it, remember that when you are getting ready for your interview.

———

For the ladies, be mindful of the amount of makeup you wear when going for an interview. As much as you can, try to keep your makeup simple as you can. If you show up with a heavily made up face, you might look attractive, but you will also be achieving two other things; calling the wrong kind of attention to yourself, and distracting your potential employers. Remember that it is important that you make the right first impression, and you certainly will not do that if you show up with a 'night out with the girls' kind of makeup.

———

Also, help yourself by making proper research about the company before you even show up. You will be able to navigate the interview better if you have some knowledge about what they are about in terms of work. Find out what the company does, learn it such that if someone wakes you up from your sleep to ask you about them, you can give reasonable answers. They expect that you bring your A game, so don't disappoint them by giving them blank looks when they ask you questions that they expect you to know the answer to. When they get to the part where they ask you if you have any question, make sure you ask an impressive question.

———

The whole point of making research beforehand is to make sure that you sound intelligent and interested in the company. Imagine that you are already working with them, and act as such.

———

Ask your interviewers questions about your work description, about the company and even about their own role in the company. You will gain their attention that way, and when you leave, they will remember who you are.

———

More often than not, there will be more than one person being interviewed for a position, all of them equally qualified for the position. Now, this qualification is on paper, so the point of an interview is to see which of all these applicants has an edge over the others and has more to deliver than what their qualification states. So, don't hold back when you are answering questions, or making a presentation as you will be doing yourself a great disservice by doing this.

———

Charisma is a very attractive quality; no wonder it is one of the knightly codes. A charismatic person is able to enter a room, hold the attention of everyone in it and leave them with a lasting impression of their presence.

———

When you enter the room where your interviewers are waiting, greet them warmly but not in a too familiar manner. Address them as Mr. or Ms., and when they extend their hand for a handshake, keep your handshake firm and maintain eye contact when you shake them. This usually translates as confidence and great social manners.

———

Ensure that your cellphone is turned off while you are at an interview. It is rude to your interviewers to have your phone ringing, or vibrating while they are interviewing you. It communicates that you don't consider the interview important enough to turn off your phone, or put it on silent mode.

———

Body language tells your interviewer a lot about you, as it speaks even louder than your voice sometimes. So you want your body language to communicate the right things- calmness, intelligence and charisma. Maintain eye contact and smile warmly. Don't slouch as that makes you look lazy- rather, sit up straight in your chair. Don't make yourself appear tense and nervous. You might feel nervous on the inside, but you don't necessarily have to show it on the outside. Some interviews are designed to make you nervous by putting you under pressure. What they are testing is how you act when placed under pressure. Will you able to withstand it, or will you crack?

Don't give them the impression that you cannot handle tension or a little pressure.

————

Another thing worthy of mention is that you are not in charge of your own interview. Don't assume the lead and start driving the interview, except if you have been given the permission to do so.

————

Your interview might turn out to be more difficult than you imagined it will be, even after preparing extensively for it. Don't let this get to you, or affect how to carry on with the interview. It might start out difficult, don't throw in your towel and just assume that it's a done deal and you can't get the job. Carry on gracefully, with the same amount of positive energy and confidence you brought in, and after the interview, thank your interviewers before you walk out. That alone can sway things in your favor.

————

Finally, if you do not know where the company is located, find out before the day of the interview. It will save you a lot of stress and prevent you from showing up late - never show up late to an interview.

———

Chapter Nine

The Principles of Chivalry When Conducting Business Over Social Media

Everything that is going down is going down on social media. It is an entire world out there, and people can literally be anything and anyone they want to be, even if that person is not their true self. Social media is both a blessing and a curse, but for the truly chivalrous person, it is a vehicle for good.

———

When going about your business on social media, no matter what that business is, make sure you hold yourself accountable and to a high standard. There might be no one to police your activities online, but do the right thing still. Whatever you put on your profile is what anyone visiting your page will take as the truth, so be very deliberate and specific about what you put on your profile. People will believe what they see on your profile. After all, you put it there. Be deliberate with your reputation and your representation of your person. You might want to go places in the future, and the only thing that will hold you back is something you said about yourself on your social media profile.

Your display pictures also say a lot about you, whether you like it or not, so be careful with what you use as your display pictures. Try as much as possible to keep nudity away from your page, especially your professional page.

Be mindful of the things you post, as they can be used against you in the future, and as much as possible, do not join the people who engage in cyber bullying. Cyber bullying has claimed lives and it has had people do despicable things to themselves and others. A truly chivalrous person avoids unwholesome acts like this like the plague.

Be mindful not to post offensive things on your social media account, or engage in aggressive discussions. If you find yourself in a discussion that is beginning to get hot, just go offline, or disengage from that discussion. These things can get nasty really quick, and you don't know when what you say in such a situation will be used against you. So many people have lost jobs over a tweet they made several years ago, either because it was racist, misogynistic, or some other form that insults a group of people, or a person.

———

A social media rule of thumb is this; if it can embarrass you or put you in a compromising position, then you should not post it. Once it is out there, it really is out. Even if you take it down from your page, what is to say that someone has not saved it already? The internet is a cold place, and if you are not careful, you can really do some serious damage to your reputation.

———

If you are running a business, and you have a social media account for it, don't mix business with your personal life. On your business page, keep it strictly business, and nothing more. Everything you post should talk about your business and other related topics. Don't post about your family, or what you did the previous night, or about how much money you spent at the club. The people that come to your page come for your business posts, don't dilute it with personal content. Open a personal page for yourself where you can talk about your life and other things. But be mindful of what you post there as well, as it could also affect your personal page. If your clients or potential clients find that you post racy comments on your personal page, they might unfollow you and your business altogether. Let your professional concerns be greater than your personal concerns, especially if your business means a lot to you- and it should.

Before you make any post on any of your social media pages, think about how the people reading it will interpret it- will it come off as potentially anti-feminist? Racist? If it will pass the message you want across the way you want it passed across, then post it. But if it will leave room for assumptions, then modify it to say exactly what you want it to say, and pass the message across the way you want it to come across.

———

Humor is not a universal language, and a true gentleman/ gentlelady understands this. Some things that are funny to you and the people around your circle might not be funny to some other people, and the internet is filled with people from all walks of life. So, be mindful of the kind of 'funny' content you post, especially if your target audience might find it offensive.

———

Be mindful of the things you like and tag people on social media. Don't associate yourself with any post that doesn't represent you or your brand well, as you could get into some form of trouble by association.

———

Another thing to remember is that you cannot afford to be overly reactive on social media. There are people that will not see your point of view on a matter, there are people that will say rude things, or even be insensitive and say very outrageous thing. But you cannot afford to become judge, jury and executioner when you see this as this is one of the ways social media spats start. As much as possible, just keep scrolling when you see things like this, unless you can react in such a way that will set off a chain of reaction that is productive, as opposed to one where a lot of insults are being passed around.

———

Too many people have all their lives on social media, every single, tiny detail of it. The chivalrous person refrains from oversharing in such a manner. Some things are just not for public consumption, and they should be kept as such; away from the public, and therefore, away from the internet. People don't need to know what you had for breakfast, lunch and the color of your poop. They sure don't need to know the tiny details of your marriage, or some private thing you did with your significant other.

In everything you do on social media, bear it in mind that you are building a legacy for the future. At some point, you may need to apply for a job, or get a grant or something, the people in charge of these things might decide to go through your social media account to get a feel of the kind of person you are. If they come across things that could incriminate you, that's the end of it. Even if you are a changed person, it will not really matter to them, as long as that evidence still exists on your page.

———

The internet provides security for a lot of people to misbehave and get away with several terrible things. People tell lies and misrepresent themselves on social media, after all, who knows they are lying? They even go as far as to use a false display picture (catfishing as it is called). A true gentleman and lady cannot be caught dead in this kind of act. They don't tell lies as such and they certainly don't create a false personality on the internet.

———

People are advised not to drink and drive, and for good reasons too. After you have had too much to drink, stay away from using any social media platform. In your state of inebriation, you might say things that could set off a chain of reaction that is unpleasant and with dire consequences.

———

A true gentleman or lady knows not to allow the false sense of security social media offers cloud their judgment and blind them from proper manners when it comes to relating with other people.

Chapter Ten

The Principles of Chivalry When Presenting a Gift for a Special Occasion

In gift gifting, know that the thought counts and something small is better than giving nothing. If you get an invite to an occasion, and it is the type for gifts, like a baby shower, wedding, bridal shower, child dedication and other such special occasions, do not show up empty handed.

———

If you cannot afford the gift of your choice, or you find yourself in a little financial fix, buy something else, no matter how small. Giving gifts goes beyond the material thing given. Gifts are more about the thought behind it, the thought that you remembered the person's special occasion, and you took time out of your schedule to buy them a gift. That amount of thoughtfulness is what is really expressed when you give a gift, and it is the most important thing. In the case that you cannot afford to buy something big, the little things count.

If the whole thing came to you in a hurry and you did not have time to pick out a gift, a gift card works as well.

If you have the time and financial resources to pick a gift, do not make the gift about you. What I mean is that a gift you are presenting to someone should be something they like, or might like, and will definitely find useful. Do not pick a gift based on something you like, or something you want to own so you automatically assume that they want it too, when in fact, they may have no use for it. If you want a gift for yourself, buy one. Just do not pick out a gift for someone based on your own preferences. Also, don't give them something that will be completely useless to them. This is more burden than gift, really.

Maybe you are not that close to them and are not sure what they will like, ask someone who you are sure will be able to answer your questions and point you in the direction of the right gift options. The person you are buying the gift for might be too polite to tell you they have no use for something you have bought them, but it's just better that you pick out something of value to them.

———

Buying gifts for someone is not an avenue to show off. Remember it is not about you, but the other person.

———

Do not break your bank account, or go above your budget when picking a gift. There will always be something good within your price range, go for those. Remember, it is the thought that counts the most.

———

Handmade gifts are still a thing, so if you can't afford to get something, just make something. Scented candle are a great example of something you can make. In fact, making your gift is also a valid option even if you can afford a gift especially if you know that such a thing is something they fancy.

———

A gentleman/ gentlelady is not someone that's stiff, they are usually creative with the things they do, and gift giving is not an exception. Don't be one to present the usual, conventional gifts all the time. Try to be creative and play around with new ideas. In fact, there are some people that if you are not creative enough, you will not be able to present them with a gift that they will actually appreciate and enjoy.

———

If you decide to give someone a gift, you should make that decision independent of whether or not the person is going to give you one in exchange. The point of giving a gift is not so that the person gives you one in return, at least, it should not be so. So, give from the goodwill of your heart, and if you get one in return, it's all well and good. If you don't, let the fact that you've made someone smile make you feel good about yourself.

————

Whatever you do, don't give someone a gift that insults their beliefs or something that they find offensive. Either on purpose or by mistake, it will still have the same effect on them. If you don't know the person well enough, ask questions from the people that do, so that you don't make such a terrible mistake. For example, if you gift a Muslim a gift card to eat for a month free at a restaurant that serves food that is not *halal*, you would have done something that insults their belief, because Muslims are not allowed to eat pork by their laws.

————

After deciding on what you want to give a person as a gift and you have purchased it, or made it, how do you present it to the person? You should not just hand the gift over to them in a bland and mundane fashion. Endeavour to have it wrapped, and placed in a gift bag before handing it over to them. Throw in a little greeting card to make it even more complete.

———

If you have been given a gift, be sure to thank the person appropriately. Send them a 'Thank you' card the next day, or a text or even a phone call, just to show that you are grateful. Even if you don't like the gift (this happens), don't act out your displeasure such that the person notices. Remember that they could have decided not to buy you a gift, so if they took the time to get you one, the least you can say is a heartfelt 'thank you'

———

If you know that it will offend the giver of a gift if you re-gift the gift they have given to you, then don't do it. In fact, I will completely advise that you don't re-gift a gift given to you. It is somewhat distasteful and inelegant.

———

Conclusion

In the wise words of Vaughn Ripley, "Chivalry is not just a fancy word with a neat meaning; it's a way of life".

Chivalry is not something you only adopt when it is convenient for you, or when you have some hidden agenda, but an actual code of life.

Make the act of chivalry a part of your life, in all possible aspects, and your life will be better off for it.

If you do not believe me, try it!